C000157546

HELP!

I'm a New Mum!

HELP!

I'm a New Mum!

3 minute prayers for new mums
...just add coffee & chocolate!

Pam Pointer

kevin mayhew

kevin mayhew

First published in Great Britain in 2017 by Kevin Mayhew Ltd
Buxhall, Stowmarket, Suffolk IP14 3BW
Tel: +44 (0) 1449 737978 Fax: +44 (0) 1449 737834
E-mail: info@kevinmayhew.com

www.kevinmayhew.com

9 8 7 6 5 4 3 2 1 0

ISBN 978 1 84867 916 0
Catalogue No. 1501554

Cover design by Rob Mortonson
© Image used under licence from Shutterstock Inc.
Edited by Helen Jones
Typeset by Angela Selfe

Printed and bound in Great Britain

Dedicated to:
Alison, Nicky and Rebecca,
three wonderful mums.

Contents

Foreword 10

About the author 11

Introduction 12

What Have We Done? 14

Too Tired 16

On the Ball 18

Squeaks and Squawks 19

Relax 20

Adam and Eve 22

Why is a Baby's Cry so Loud? 24

Exhausted 26

God 28

Apprehensive 30

Tears 32

Joy 34

Still in My Pyjamas 36

Funny Peculiar 38

Helpless 40

A Little Bit Lonely   42

Expectations   44

Conflicting Advice   46

Social Media   48

The Art of Dressing   50

Sleep Deprivation   52

Learning to Play   56

First Outing   60

The Midwife   62

Tiny Toes to Button Nose   64

Life Changes   66

The Things I Miss   68

Fun   70

One Day at a Time   72

Returning to Work   74

Thank You For My Baby   76

Guardians of Treasure   78

My Parents   80

First Smile   82

In Special Circumstances

Emergency C-Section   84

Early Arrival   86

Perfection   88

Adoption   90

And Finally …

The CV of a One-Year-Old   92

Foreword

Being a mum is not all coffee mornings, cake and manicures. Every time I thought I was getting the hang of things, the routine would change. It could be teething, a growth spurt or just a runny nose but these things all knocked any routine and my confidence with it.

We can be driven to our knees by the sheer wonder of the new life we now care for, or from the utter despair of not knowing how to get through another day on so little sleep.

Being a new mum is hard! It's all unknown. Only the other day I explained to my younger daughter, when she asked, that training to be a mum isn't something you can do at university.

And yet we have a God who loves us deeply and is longing for us to share all of our life with him. We can tell him how we really feel. And often it's when we pour out the struggles and uncertainty, that the cloud starts to lift and the despair turns to joy and hope, and we are renewed and more able to keep going.

Pam Pointer's years of experience as a mother, and now as a grandmother supporting her three daughters as they become new mothers themselves, shines through in this collection of prayers to help new mums find words for every occasion. Her empathetic approach gives these prayers a healthy dose of realism, understanding and wisdom.

Being a mum is an amazing adventure and time goes quickly, so relish every moment.

Nicky Edwards
Mum of two daughters who bring so much delight; the rest fades away.

About the author

Pam is a writer, speaker and photographer whose work reflects her observations of the natural world and its human inhabitants.

Why Didn't God Create Me With Green Hair? was Pam's first book, published in 1999. She has written a number of other books, plus many magazine articles on subjects as diverse as sleeping on the pavement in the Wimbledon queue, the work of hospital chaplains, and the merit of cows. She has contributed columns to local and national newspapers, broadcast morning thoughts for local radio, written an RE syllabus and teaching outlines, and writes meditations for an international magazine.

Pam is married with three daughters, three sons-in-law and five grandchildren. She enjoys being a homemaker, walking in the countryside, watching period drama on TV, blogging on her website: https://pampointer.wordpress.com/, and listening to 1960s rock music, Classic FM and Test Match Special.

Pam is passionate about God, and Jesus is the solid rock on which her life is built.

Introduction

Help! I'm a New Mum! is a gift book of prayers for new mums as they face the adventure of looking after a baby.

'Lord, I sometimes wonder what we've done ...' Maybe, as a new mum, you're wondering just that! It's the opening phrase of the first prayer in *Help! I'm a New Mum!* A young woman expresses her thoughts aloud to God immediately following the birth of her child, and ponders the future changes that will affect the lives of all concerned. The prayers that follow trace the ups and downs of life with a new little being who, for the first few weeks, is unable to communicate other than in tricky-to-interpret cries and wriggles, until that magical moment of the first smile when the mum feels she's beginning to get the hang of being a mother. No two days are the same, however, so weigh-day and play times, feeding and changing times present new challenges and adventures during the first days, weeks and months with a new baby. These activities and the emotions that accompany them are all expressed in the prayers.

Prayers can sometimes be too polite, too politically correct, too pious or just plain dull. Does God yawn when he hears them, or despair that we're not being real in our communication with him? Like many of the Psalms, *Help! I'm a New Mum!* bucks any churchy trend for polite prayers. Whether or not you have a faith, it's quite likely that you'll call out to God for help, or to say thank you, or to vent your frustration because you're at the end of your tether. The prayers are expressed in contemporary language with honesty and vigour. If you're a busy mum, too frazzled to think of what to say to God, *Help! I'm a New Mum!* will be a useful tool for expressing thoughts to God in an unstuffy and refreshing way. The prayers are complemented by short quotes from the Bible and other sources.

Help! I'm a New Mum! is a book to have by your bed or by the kettle. Dip into the book and find the right prayer for whatever situation you find yourself in. Ultimately the joy and privilege of being a mother is paramount, and there is plenty of scope to thank God for his provision and his presence through all the drama of motherhood.

The words may bring smiles or tears, reassurance or an epiphany moment of thinking, 'Yes, that's just how I feel.'

What Have We Done?

Lord, I sometimes wonder what we've done!
It all seemed so easy when there was just the bump,
even though those last weeks were uncomfortable.
You know, Lord, how I wondered whether I would
cope with labour and delivery.
I did, Lord, with your help.
But it was hard work and very painful
and I'm not sure I'd want to do all that again.

And then there was baby,
this little life that you entrusted to us.
This tiny being, perfectly formed in your image
for us to care for on your behalf.
To think that I am responsible for meeting his needs
is awesome and scary.

When I'm tired and feel like screaming as he does,
help him to know that he is still loved.
When I long for just a few minutes of respite from him,
help him to know that he is precious.
When I find it hard to feed him,
when I'm sore,
when I have to tickle the soles of his feet
to keep him awake enough to feed,
when I long for him to sleep so I can too,
when his bottom has exploded over everything,
and his top has sicked up what I fed him,

when the tank of tears regularly spills down
my cheeks,
when I fear that I'm inadequate for the task,
when I realise that this is not a temporary role,
when I feel panicky...
Just remind me that you love me, Lord;
remind me that I'm yours,
that I too am special
and precious
and infinitely loved by you
just as I am,
full of tempestuous hormones,
not understanding myself,
trying to put on a brave and calm front
when underneath I fear I'm not coping...

Then, Lord, flood me with your peace,
hold me and protect me in your arms,
and remind me that, together, we can do it.
You and me, Lord, working in partnership,
along with those who love and care for me:
my husband, parents, sisters and friends.
Remind me that this little baby doesn't just depend on
me and those closest to me,
but that he can depend on the maker of the universe,
on the only perfect parent
who never makes mistakes,
whose arms are open in welcome
and who loves my baby
even more than I do.
Thank you, Lord.

Too Tired

Lord, I'm too tired to talk to you today.
In hospital our baby was snuggled in her little cot by
my side,
cocooned in her blanket,
and seemed quite content.

When we brought her home
she took an instant dislike to her Moses basket
and I ended up sitting all night holding her,
marvelling at this tiny little person
who'd come into our lives
but wondering whether I'd have to sit up with her
every night for ever and ever.
Consequently, I'm tired.

In fact, I'm too tired to talk to anyone.
I don't even feel like talking to my husband.
Thank you that he's so understanding.
He just gets on with putting the bins out
and doing the washing up
and reassuring me that labour meant labour
and labour's tiring.
Well, he may not know about the baby-kind of labour
but he certainly works hard.
I'm grateful for him,
and for him just holding me when I'm too tired to talk.
Please will you just hold me too?

I expect plenty of other people are talking to you
so you won't mind me being silent for once.
I can't say another word.
I'll be in touch again very soon no doubt.

[Jesus said] 'Come to me, all of you who are tired
from carrying heavy loads, and I will give you rest.'
Matthew 11:28

The Lord is the everlasting God;
he created all the world.
He never grows tired or weary ...
He strengthens those
who are weak and tired ...
But those who trust in the Lord
for help will find their strength renewed.
They will rise
on wings like eagles;
they will run and not get weary;
they will walk and not grow weak.
Isaiah 40:28-31

On the Ball

It's me again, Lord.
I'd expect you, Lord God, to get tired.
You did all that creation work at the beginning
of time,
then had to contend with the rebellion of the people
you'd created.
You planned, then carried out a rescue.
No wonder we call you Almighty God!
I'm tired with one baby – you've had squillions!
And you never get tired?
Never get weary?
Well, it's a good thing one of us is on the ball
and it's definitely not me.
Thank you that not only do you never get tired,
but you take the time to strengthen us
and set us going again
and again,
and again.

The Lord reached down from above
and took hold of me.
Psalm 18:16

Squeaks and Squawks

Am I naive, Lord?
I had no idea that having this so-called bundle of joy
could be so exhausting,
so bewildering and so scary.
Here I am with this wriggling, squealing baby,
and I don't know what she's trying to tell me.
I'm not used to someone speaking in squeaks
and squawks
and yelps and yells and wordless babble.
It makes me feel like when I was at school
and my French teacher gabbled away
and I hadn't a clue what she was saying
despite her theatrical gestures.
Well, the theatrical gestures from my baby
are her arm waving and knee bends
and gummy mouth opening and closing,
none of which helps me interpret the noise
she makes.
Help me to be calm when I feel anxious (which is
most of the time),
to try and relax when I feel tense (ditto most of
the time),
and to accept that my bundle of joy has off moments
and off days just as I do.

Relax

Relax.
I'm tense today,
'Relax!' they say,
but tension grips
with vicious clips;
I'm so hard-pressed
with constant stress,
muscles tight,
knuckles white,
head bent down,
pout and frown;
'Relax!' they say;
Relax? No way!
Twiddle thumbs,
fingers drum.

Close the door,
relax your jaw,
stretch your hands
like rubber bands,
smooth your face,
slow your pace;
try a smile
for a while;
still your mind,
just unwind;
blot out fear,
peace is near.

Shut your eyes,
see blue skies,
tranquil seas,
gentle breeze;
pleasant things
peace, joy brings;
calm your will;
then be still.

Be still,
stay still,
still,
yes, still;
listen ...
to the silent whisper
of God
and be at peace.

Adam and Eve

Dear God, I can't help feeling that Adam and Eve
have a lot to answer for.
Can I have your permission to blame them
for those excruciating labour pains
and the trauma of giving birth?
Or should I blame you,
for it was you who, after Adam and Eve's bodge-up,
declared that women would suffer in childbirth.
How right you were.
And how!
Now I know why my own mother
dislikes watching TV dramas showing labour and
childbirth.
Those actresses certainly know how to yell.

You even say in the Bible that all of creation groans
with pain,
like the pain of childbirth.
There's so much pain and anguish, Lord,
and I guess my temporary pain in labour is trivial
compared with the agony of the world's pain.
So instead of blaming Adam and Eve and you,
I should remember what the 'experts' say.
They tell me the nightmare memories of labour and
birth will fade,
and that plenty of women go on to have another child
or two, or even ten!
My health visitor told me she was one of ten.

What a thought.
Which makes me say thank God for just one.

So Lord, in good moments,
I do indeed thank you – without yelling –
for this amazing little life.

God said, 'And now we will make human beings;
they will be like us and resemble us …' God created
human beings, making them to be like himself.
He created them male and female, blessed them
and said, 'Have many children …' God looked at
everything he had made, and he was very pleased.
Genesis 1:26-28, 31

[God] said to the woman, 'I will increase your trouble
in pregnancy and your pain in giving birth.'
Genesis 3:16

Tears may flow in the night,
but joy comes in the morning.
Psalm 30:5

One of the shortest journeys in the world – a baby's
trip down the birth canal – is also one of the most
important: the infant's entrance onto the stage of life.

Why is a Baby's Cry so Loud?

Dear Lord, sometimes I feel I'd like to change my
baby for a quieter model.
But as he's not a vacuum cleaner
or a washing machine, I guess I can't.
My sister says her baby is scared of the
vacuum cleaner
even though it has a happy face on it.
It's the thunderous noise it makes.
As for the washing machine...
Well, mine has always made its presence felt.
The monster in the corner I call it.

Why is a baby's cry so LOUD?
It's just that when he bawls
and carries on bawling,
and I don't know what to do to pacify him,
then I think ...
But no, this is the one you've given us.

Here is the miracle of birth,
of new life,
a life of opportunity and adventure,
challenge and toil,
joy and sorrow,
noise and ... quiet
if I'm lucky.

You calm the roar of the seas
and the noise of the waves;
you calm the uproar of the peoples.
Psalm 65:7

Show us, good Lord,
the peace we should seek,
the peace we must give,
the peace we must keep,
the peace we must forego,
and the peace you have
given us in Jesus our Lord.
Anonymous

The Lord is my shepherd; I have everything I need.
He lets me rest in fields of green grass
and leads me to quiet pools of fresh water.
He gives me new strength.
Psalm 23:1-3

May the Lord bless you and take care of you;
May the Lord be kind and gracious to you;
May the Lord look on you with favour
and give you peace.
Numbers 6:24-26

Exhausted

Lord, I'm exhausted.
My brain seems to have switched off
or maybe gone onto a kind of minimal autopilot.
Do you remember Job, Lord?
He had a terrible time of it.
'Teach us what to say to God,' I read in the Bible.
'Our minds are blank; we have nothing to say.'
I know that feeling.
I'm too tired to think.
Fill my mind with your wisdom.
At the moment it's so befuddled I hardly know
which day it is,
or even what time of day I've reached.
How long will this exhaustion last?

I am worn out, O Lord; have pity on me! Give me
strength; I am completely exhausted and my whole
being is deeply troubled … I am worn out with grief;
every night my bed is damp from my weeping;
my pillow is soaked with tears.

Psalm 6:2, 3, 6

I said, 'I am falling';
but your constant love, O Lord, held me up.

Psalm 94:18

My help will come from the Lord, who made
heaven and earth. He will not let you fall;
your protector is always awake. The protector of
Israel never dozes or sleeps. The Lord will guard
you; he is by your side to protect you.
Psalm 121:2-5

In the muddle and mayhem of an occupied town
overrun with tired travellers, Jesus was born –
Emmanuel, meaning God is with us. Jesus Christ,
in his humanity, knows all about weariness,
hopes and fears, and in his divinity is able to
meet them with calm and compassion.

God

God ...
Chooses to dwell where heaven meets earth,
living in both as Emmanuel.
Comes close beside me, in front of me, behind me,
above me, within me.
Cares for me more than anybody on earth ever
could or would want to.
Carries me when I'm too weary to walk or too
troubled to talk.
Caresses me when I'm sad, hugs me tight and lets
my tears splash on him.
Calms me as I walk in his hills and in woods,
as I listen to him in birdsong.
Challenges me to keep him as my focus when I'm so
easily distracted.
Cheers me all the way through life's marathon, and
then helps me over the line.

Apprehensive

Lord, I'm apprehensive.
I've been apprehensive before,
like when I went to a new school.
There I was in my new over-sized uniform,
trying to remember where to get off the bus,
wondering if I'd find my way round all the rooms,
feeling scared of new teachers ...

And when I started my first job,
doing the commute,
trying to understand new systems,
meeting new people ...
Scary stuff.

But this; this is totally different.
Suddenly I'm responsible for a new living being.

I managed to master machines and technology
most of the time,
but now I'm looking after a real live person
who didn't choose to have me for a mother!
And I wonder if I can cope.

Can we do it together, Lord,
as a foursome,
my husband and me,
our baby and you?

I have cared for you from the time you were born.
I am your God and will take care of you
until you are old and your hair is grey.
I made you and will care for you.
Isaiah 46:3, 4

Do not be afraid – I am with you!
Isaiah 43:5

I am the Lord who created you;
from the time you were born, I have helped you.
Isaiah 44:2

He will take care of his flock like a shepherd;
he will gather the lambs together and carry them
in his arms; he will gently lead their mothers.
Isaiah 40:11

Tears

I can't remember the last time I cried every day, Lord.
There have been times of grief in my life
and times of disappointment and fear when
I've cried,
but this is different.
Sometimes my tears come suddenly and
unexpectedly
and take me by surprise;
I suppose it's my hormones
that haven't quite decided
what my state of play is
and so haven't adjusted
to the new post-birth me.
Other times the tears come when my baby won't
feed properly
or when her nappy has burst out everywhere
and I have to clear up the mess.

I'm bewildered, Lord.
There we were, my husband and I,
looking forward to the arrival of our first child,
but then reality hit in the form of this tiny baby
and my emotions are all over the place.
How could something we longed for
be causing me so much confusion and panic?
Don't get me wrong, Lord.

I'm very grateful for our baby,
but baffled by my mixed feelings,
my inability to cope
and my concerns about whether I'll ever be able to
be a good mum.
Will it get better, Lord?

They say I'll look back on it one day
and have a good laugh
but at present it doesn't seem very funny.
They say that laughter and tears are very close.
Funny isn't it that our eyes leak
with both amusement and anxiety.
But not at the same time.

When the Lord saw her, his heart was filled with
pity for her, and he said to her, 'Don't cry.'
Luke 7:13

Be confident, my heart, because the Lord has been
good to me. The Lord saved me from death;
he stopped my tears and kept me from defeat.
And so I walk in the presence of the Lord
in the world of the living.
Psalm 116:7-9

He will wipe away all tears from their eyes. There will
be no more death, no more grief or crying or pain.
Revelation 21:4

Joy

Joy comes in the morning.
Tears of night subside
as morning dawns
and creation wakes
to dance to the rhythm of day
on heather hillsides,
through whispering woods
and on shushing shingle shores.

Lord, in nature's movements
you hint at a new creation day,
when Paradise will be restored.
So today I wake, content
and at peace in your presence,
and wait with hope
as you fill me with joy.

Still in My Pyjamas

I've reverted to being a teenager, Lord.
Do you remember
when I'd stay in bed on Saturday mornings until
11 o'clock?
Was it because I was genuinely tired
or was it the hormonal stuff?
Hormones – never easy.
So what is it now?
Hormones?
No, I don't think so.
Just an inability to get everything done.

Here I am in the middle of the day,
still in my pyjamas
because I just haven't had time to get dressed.
And I'm longing to jump in the shower,
wash my hair,
fit into a skirt …

How long will I have a saggy, baggy tummy?

Was it only a few weeks ago that I was
smartly dressed,
going to work,
being efficient in my job,
wearing heels and make-up?
It seems a lifetime ago.

Lord, you have examined me and you know me.
You know everything I do; from far away you
understand all my thoughts. You see me, whether
I am working or resting; you know all my actions.
Even before I speak, you already know what I
will say ... Your knowledge of me is too deep;
it is beyond my understanding.

Psalm 139:1-4, 6

The Lord said to [Samuel], 'Pay no attention to how
tall and handsome he is ... I do not judge as people
judge. They look at the outward appearance,
but I look at the heart.'

1 Samuel 16:7

Clothe yourselves with compassion, kindness,
humility, gentleness, and patience.

Colossians 3:12

Funny Peculiar

It's funny, Lord, funny peculiar.
I have to learn to feed my baby,
just as I had to learn to read,
mastering letters and the illogical spellings of
English words.
There, their, they're.
Huh, that's what you say to pacify someone.
I need pacifying these days.

And learning to drive:
Mirror, signal, action.
'It's all good fun, changing up and down,'
my instructor used to say
when I was clunking the gears to leap-frog forwards.
It required such mental and physical agility –
multi-tasking, I suppose.

Mothers are supposed to be good at multi-tasking.
Well, maybe this feeding lark will become natural;
it isn't at the moment.
And there's all the pressure
from those who say breast is best
and look down their noses at those who bottle-feed.
I'll just have to do my best at feeding my baby,
as I did with learning to read and learning to drive.

Help me to be patient and to persevere
and to remember that, when you and I look at adults,
we can't tell which ones were breast-fed
and which were bottle-fed.
Actually, *you* can because you know everything
but I can't and I guess it doesn't matter anyway.

We feast on the abundant food you provide;
you let us drink from the river of your goodness.
You are the source of all life.
Psalm 36:8, 9

All living things look hopefully to you, and you give
them food when they need it. You give them
enough and satisfy the needs of all.
Psalm 145:15, 16

Love is patient and kind.
1 Corinthians 13:4

Do all the good you can,
By all the means you can,
In all the ways you can,
In all the places you can,
At all the times you can,
To all the people you can,
As long as ever you can.
Attributed to John Wesley 1703-91

Helpless

Lord, sometimes I feel as helpless as my baby.
Can I just have a moment
to lie on the floor
and kick my legs
and wave my arms
and pretend that I don't have to do anything
other than just be?
Can someone else take over for a bit?

I have to learn to receive from other people
and I'm so grateful for the people who've brought
us meals,
hoovered the floor,
hung out the washing,
done the ironing,
been to the supermarket –
all the things I used to do without a second thought
except perhaps for the ironing
which always needs a second
or third thought before it's tackled.

There seem to be lots of lovely people out there
who are ready to lend a hand;
many of them have been through this baby stage
so they're very understanding but,
better than that,
they're practical!

Help carry one another's burdens.
Galatians 6:2

Let us give thanks to the God and Father of our Lord Jesus Christ, the merciful Father, the God from whom all help comes! He helps us in all our troubles, so that we are able to help others who have all kinds of troubles, using the same help that we ourselves have received from God.
2 Corinthians 1:3, 4

Encourage one another and help one another.
1 Thessalonians 5:11

Do not forget to do good and to help one another.
Hebrews 13:16

A Little Bit Lonely

When I was at work, Lord, I was surrounded by
other people.
Sometimes I resented the nearness of other
people's desks,
the constant whirr of computers,
the incessant phone calls.
On the whole, though, it was good
and I enjoyed being with other people.
Now I'm here at home with a baby.

I can't talk to him about the internet
or my clients or the FTSE or government policies.
Or could I?
Would my baby know the difference
between me talking about toys and teddy bears,
or conference calls and competition?

To be honest, Lord, I feel a bit lonely,
I miss my colleagues,
and I wonder whether this motherhood thing is
really for me.
Of course it is.
We planned it!
We wanted it.
We're glad of it – I think.

Help me to accept my new responsibilities as a
big adventure
and to be excited at the prospect
of bringing up my baby to take his part in the world.

Do your work, not for mere pay, but from a real desire to serve. Do not try to rule over those who have been put in your care, but be examples ... All of you must put on the apron of humility, to serve one another.

1 Peter 5:2, 3, 5

Turn to me, Lord, and be merciful to me, because I am lonely and weak.

Psalm 25:16

[Jesus said] 'I will be with you always.'

Matthew 28:20

Bonding sessions have become a popular feature of the workplace. When you're at home with a baby, it's a different kind of bonding that you work at. After months inside the womb, baby is now out in the bewildering world of colour, light, noise, texture, taste and touch, and has much to learn. Bonding with baby is a special privilege and role, but so is finding adult company! Baby and toddler groups are a great way to exchange news and views and even have some grown up conversation. You may or may not wish to follow the example of the father who, apparently, always talked to his baby as if he were talking to his bank manager!

Expectations

Lord, our expectations were a bit unrealistic.
We expected to be able to carry on as we had before.
You know the sort of thing, Lord.
As it was in the beginning, is now,
and ever shall be,
world without end.
Although actually that would be very boring.
Life has to be adventurous, doesn't it?

Little did we realise that our life would be
changed forever
(although plenty of people told us it would).
It's been a bit of a shock
and I guess no book
nor the wise words of people who've been through
this before us,
could ever fully prepare us for parenthood.

I never really noticed my parents' parenting.
I suppose they did it.
I just took it for granted
so didn't bother to learn from their example.
I want to be a good mum,
to love my baby,
to bring baby up to enjoy life
and to contribute to the lives of others.
Help me to have sensible expectations
and to set realistic goals.

Jesus Christ is the same yesterday, today, and forever.

Hebrews 13:8

Through all the changing scenes of life,
in trouble and in joy,
the praises of my God shall still
my heart and tongue employ.

Nahum Tate (1652-1715) and Nicholas Brady (1659-1726)

For he is our childhood's pattern;
Day by day, like us He grew;
He was little, weak and helpless,
Tears and smiles like us He knew;
And He feeleth for our sadness,
And He shareth in our gladness.

Cecil Frances Alexander (1818-95)

Each family is a miniature version of God's family. His parental love and care can be demonstrated in each human family where everyone of all ages and different generations lives and moves in harmony. A family is never static. Its members should move together like waves on the ocean or leaves on the tree. Each member has an individual personality but is part of the whole. It's exciting to watch baby find his feet (literally and metaphorically) as he grows and learns and realises he's part of something that we call family.

Conflicting Advice

Why, Lord, am I receiving so much conflicting advice?
Who knows best?
Everyone seems to have an opinion
about anything
and everything
and thinks they should share it with me!
Anyone from the health visitor and doctor
to the lady next door
and the cashier at the supermarket checkout.
Not to mention my mother
and my mother-in-law
(Ooh, watch this space on those two!)
I'm sure they all mean well.
They probably see my struggles
and it's rather touching that people want to help
each other.

The Bible says that sensible people accept advice.
I hope I'm sensible, but whose advice should I accept?
It's very confusing!
Should I just trust my instinct?

Each of us is different, a unique individual. God knew
us before we were born; he knows the number of
hairs on our head, and each person is of immense
value to him. God's love is universal and his care

constant, but he deals with us as individuals, loving, caring, correcting, guiding, comforting and challenging us.

A midwife recalls the 62 babies she had delivered. Each miraculous event was thrilling and scary but, she says, 'Having a baby myself came as something of a shock. I had the knowledge and the know-how but had no idea what it was really like to give birth until I did so myself.' Guide books, health visitors, friends, family members, can all give different advice. 'Choose one person whose advice you value – or just trust your instincts!' she says.

Social Media

Was it a mistake, Lord, to post on social media
about my baby's sleep pattern
or lack of pattern?
I'm increasingly uneasy about social media.
So many nasty threads,
so much gossip,
and do we really need to know
the itsy-bitsy details of everyone's life?
But I'm just as bad!
I do it too!
Anyway, the 23 'likes'
and 17 comments I've had are all different,
so make me more baffled than ever.
And that's just my friends.
I'm bombarded by internet advisers,
healthcare professionals,
government rules and regulations
all telling me what I should and shouldn't do,
the how, what, when, where,
of bringing up a baby.
So many opinions.

I'm in danger of repeating myself
in these chats with you, Lord.
Here I go again:
Perhaps I should just trust my instincts
and muddle through.
Help me, Lord!

[God said to Joshua,] 'Remember that I have commanded you to be determined and confident! Do not be afraid or discouraged, for I, the Lord your God, am with you wherever you go.'

Joshua 1:9

Don't fret if you can't fold a fitted sheet or are completely inept at programming your phone or don't know how to make your baby sleep. As for friends on Facebook … Living in the internet age of computer-generated communication can actually make us feel isolated and lonely because there is less personal contact with other people. But however lonely we may be – and for whatever reasons – God's promise is that he is always there to listen. It's all about relationship. Get to know God as the best and most communicative friend ever.

The Art of Dressing

Lord, I couldn't ever have imagined how tricky it is
dressing something that moves all the time.
It's just possible that Adam and Eve were onto a
good thing
when you put them in the garden naked.
And then things went pear-shaped
or apple-shaped
or whatever the fruit was on that tree.
And you provided them with clothes.
You even made them!
I suppose they got used to clothes after that.
And were glad of the extra warmth.

My efforts with my baby are laughable.
I understand why the necks of vests are designed as
they are
but even so, trying to get the largest part of the baby
– its head –
through the gap
is no mean feat.

Then comes the Babygro.
Lord, I'm so grateful for the person who told me
to start popping the Babygro from the bottom up
rather than from the top down.
What a brilliant invention!
And what good advice!

Now my baby's snug
until the next time
when we have another practise session
on the art of dressing.

She gave birth to her first son, wrapped him in
cloths and laid him in a manger.
Luke 2:7

Jesus said to the disciples, 'And so I tell you not
to worry about the food you need to stay alive
or about the clothes you need for your body. Life
is much more important than food, and the body
much more important than clothes ... Look how the
wild flowers grow: they don't work or make clothes
for themselves. But I tell you that not even King
Solomon with all his wealth had clothes as beautiful
as one of these flowers. It is God who clothes
the wild grass – grass that is here today and gone
tomorrow, burned up in the oven. Won't he be all the
more sure to clothe you? What little faith you have!'
Luke 12:22, 23, 27, 28

So the Lord answers, 'Can a woman forget her
own baby and not love the child she bore? Even if
a mother should forget her child, I will never forget
you. Jerusalem, I can never forget you! I have
written your name on the palms of my hands.'
Isaiah 49:15, 16

Sleep Deprivation

A bad night, Lord.
I remember bad nights when I was a child.
The recurring nightmare of a man
chasing me through woods and me running
and running,
trying to escape his clutches.
Then I'd wake, shaking with fear.
Or the times when I woke with tummy ache
and felt sick.
Or later, when I was much older,
waking in fear and trepidation
because of an exam the next day.
But on the whole, back then, I slept well.

I now know what they mean by sleep deprivation.
Like in those awful torture chambers
where lights are kept on all night
and the prisoner forced to keep awake.
Lord, it's silly for me to compare my situation
with torture.
Having a crying baby isn't torture
but the crying does seem worse in the night.

Thank you for the kind people who've said
I can phone them any time,
day or night, for reassurance.
(I do feel a bit guilty at phoning my sister at 2.30am,

but she was OK about it – and made me feel a
bit better.)
My sister has been so kind, Lord.
She's finished the baby stage with her two
but remembers how difficult she found those
first weeks.
You muddle through, she says,
and do your best
even though you're worn out with the effort!
She sends hugs in envelopes
along with a lot of one-line jokes.
She texts and emails and phones
and keeps me smiling.
Thank you, Lord, for sisters!

For there is no friend like a sister
In calm or stormy weather;
To cheer one on the tedious way,
To fetch one if one goes astray,
To lift one if one totters down,
To strengthen whilst one stands.
Christina Rossetti 1830-94

A ministering angel shall my sister be.
William Shakespeare 1564-1616

Even darkness is not dark for you, and the
night is as bright as the day. Darkness and
light are the same to you.
Psalm 139:12

As I lie in bed, I remember you; all night long I think of you, because you have always been my help. In the shadow of your wings I sing for joy. I cling to you, and your hand keeps me safe.

Psalm 63:6-8

There shall be no more night, and they will not need lamps or sunlight, because the Lord God will be their light.

Revelation 22:5

But you do see; you take notice of trouble and suffering and are always ready to help. The helpless commit themselves to you; you have always helped the needy ... You will listen, O Lord, to the prayers of the lowly; you will give them courage.

Psalm 10:14, 17

Learning to Play

Lord, I need to learn how to play.
I can play tennis,
I can play cards,
but I have to learn now, Lord,
how to play with my baby.
I can shake a rattle,
wave Teddy's paw at him,
sing nursery rhymes
(when I can remember the words)
and read him a book.
I felt a bit silly at first reading to him
all about farm animals
but I felt my tension fall away
as I made mooing noises
and woofed at my baby!

Some of the nursery rhymes have alarming lyrics.
Down will come baby, cradle and all …
Cut off their tails with a carving knife …
Pecked off her nose …
Good thing my baby can't understand words yet.
Makes me smile, Lord, just to think of it.

I'd prefer my baby to sleep at night
and play in the daytime!
Apparently babies enjoy music
and aren't concerned about whether my singing
is particularly tuneful.

The soothing sound of my voice
and some gentle movement
is enough to start with,
though some of these ancient rhymes,
like some fairy tales,
have weird and eyebrow-raising words:
Hush-a-bye baby; Ding dong bell; Three blind mice ...
Maybe I'll stick with 'The Wheels on the Bus'.

The reward for singing
and playing with my baby
will come as baby makes eye contact with me,
squirms with delight,
smiles a gummy smile
and gurgles in baby talk back to me.
I guess it won't be long before
my child is singing
and dancing
and playing games
and winning against me ...

Children run and play like lambs and dance
to the music of harps and flutes.
Job 21:11, 12

Praise the Lord! Praise God in his Temple!
Praise his strength in heaven!
Praise him for the mighty things he has done.
Praise his supreme greatness.
Praise him with trumpets.
Praise him with harps and lyres.
Praise him with drums and dancing.
Praise him with harps and flutes.
Praise him with cymbals.
Praise him with loud cymbals.
Praise the Lord, all living creatures!
Praise the Lord!
Psalm 150

Homes are built on the foundation of
wisdom and understanding.
Proverbs 24:3

'Let the children come to me, and do not
stop them, because the Kingdom of God
belongs to such as these.'
Luke 18:16

First Outing

We had our first outing today, Lord.
Driving a buggy is different to driving a car.
Not so many actions required
but I still had to think.
First, I had to get the baby ready:
extra clothes,
a hat,
blanket
and rain cover – just in case.
By the time I'd done all that,
I was ready to sit down again.
But I persevered
and we walked down the road
and back again.

I was out of the house for
all of ten minutes
and it felt like an hour.
We did it
and oh, Lord,
the feeling of achievement.
Now for a lie-down …

A journey of a thousand miles begins
with a single step.
Lao Tzu (Ancient Chinese Philosopher)

He who is outside his door already has the hardest
part of his journey behind him.
(Dutch proverb)

He that is down needs fear no fall,
He that is low, no pride;
He that is humble ever shall
Have God to be his guide.
I am content with what I have,
Little be it or much;
And, Lord, contentment still I crave,
Because Thou savest such.
Fullness to such a burden is
That go on pilgrimage;
Here little, and hereafter bliss,
Is best from age to age.
John Bunyan 1628-88 (From The Pilgrim's Progress)

The Midwife

The midwife came today, Lord, to weigh my baby.
You know how it is, Lord, with scales.
With me, I step on very gingerly,
work out which way I need to lean
to make them read the lightest possible weight
then chastise myself if I've put on a few pounds.
But it's different with my baby.
I want her to gain weight not lose it.
I'm on tenterhooks.
My baby lost weight to start with
and I know that's normal.
But she doesn't seem to be gaining much weight
so I hope she's OK.

The midwife will come again in a couple of days.
And we'll repeat the process:
Undressing,
waiting for the wail as baby is left starkers and cold
then dressing her again.
And giving her a big hug.
Breathing a sigh of relief when the health
visitor leaves.

But thank you, Lord,
for these health professionals
who have my baby's best interests at heart.

The intricacies of the human body are mind-boggling – 150,000km of peripheral nerves ... thousands of taste buds ... and 50 little muscles that crisscross the face and head, making it possible for us to smile, grimace, question, express surprise or look sympathetic ... and a brain to appreciate it, wonder at it, and thank God for it.

Children are a gift from the Lord;
they are a real blessing.
Psalm 127:3

Hope returns when I remember this one thing:
The Lord's unfailing love and mercy still continue,
Fresh as the morning, as sure as the sunrise.
Lamentations 3:21-23

Tiny Toes to Button Nose

I've had a good day today, Lord.
Most of the time, anyway.
I actually got dressed before lunchtime,
even if only in my jogging bottoms
and a baggy T-shirt
which are the only clothes
that are comfortable at the moment.

I've had time to make some lunch,
just a cheese sandwich and coffee,
but it was good, oh so good.
I even washed up afterwards before
the round of
feeding,
burping,
changing,
sleeping,
started all over again.

My lunch and his lunch!
Both achieved
without too many hitches,
and I've even managed
a couple of catnaps myself.
Hooray!

And now, Lord, please excuse me whispering to you.
I seldom whisper.

The thing is, all is quiet at the moment.
I don't want to spoil the silence by talking aloud.
I love the peace of this moment.

I'm gazing at my sleeping baby, Lord,
and he's lovely.
From his tiny toes to his button nose …
What a miraculous creation.

Who else but you, Lord,
could have thought up such a wonderful and
intricate design.
We humans think we're so clever
but after thousands of years
we still haven't sussed out
all there is to know about the human body.
I'm glad you know it all!

I will praise you, Lord, with all my heart;
I will tell of all the wonderful things you have done.
I will sing with joy because of you.
I will sing praise to you, Almighty God.
Psalm 9:1, 2

As a child lies quietly in its mother's arms,
so my heart is quiet within me.
Psalm 131:2

Now at last the whole world enjoys rest and peace,
and everyone sings for joy.
Isaiah 14:7

Life Changes

I couldn't imagine, Lord, that my life would change
so much
and it's only beginning to dawn on me now
that I'm in this role for life,
that motherhood isn't like the other jobs I've had
which I could leave when I chose to
and do something else.

It's weird to think that my baby may,
one day,
be a mother herself,
but she'll still call me Mum.

Help me to look after her
and care for her
so that our relationship of mother and daughter
may blossom and flourish
for as long as we both live.

The Lord says, 'Do not cling to events of the past
or dwell on what happened long ago. Watch for the
new thing I am going to do. It is happening already –
you can see it now! I will make a road through the
wilderness and give you streams of water there.'

Isaiah 43:18, 19

Everything that happens in this world
happens at the time God chooses.

Ecclesiastes 3:1

All the world's a stage,
And all the men and women merely players;
They have their exits and their entrances,
And one man in his time plays many parts,
His acts being seven ages.

William Shakespeare (1564-1616)

[Jesus said] 'Peace is what I leave with you;
it is my own peace that I give you. I do not give
it as the world does. Do not be worried
and upset; do not be afraid.'

John 14:27

The Things I Miss

Lord, I didn't think I was selfish, or self-centred,
until our baby arrived.
Then, Lord, I found that I couldn't do what I wanted
or, that as a married couple,
we couldn't choose to go where we wanted
when we wanted.
I miss going to the theatre
without a care in the world,
miss our lengthy conversations
about life and the universe.
We're lucky if we have five minutes
of grown-up chat these days,
and the thought of going on a date
with my husband seems too hard to organise
at the moment
and I'd probably fall asleep anyway.

We have someone else to consider now,
and I realise that the smallest one in the family
will impact our lives.
Help us to build a life as a family,
to enjoy the things we can do together,
to have adventures
and to know that one day
we'll be missing our 'baby'
who has grown up
and left us free to have

those long conversations
and theatre outings
whenever we want.

Decide today whom you will serve …
As for my family and me, we will serve the Lord.
Joshua 24:15

The Lord says … 'Share your food with the hungry
and open your homes to the homeless poor. Give
clothes to those who have nothing to wear, and
do not refuse to help your own relatives. Then my
favour will shine on you like the morning sun, and
your wounds will be quickly healed. I will always be
with you to save you; my presence will protect you
on every side. When you pray, I will answer you.
When you call to me, I will respond.'
Isaiah 58:7-9

Teach children how they should live,
and they will remember it all their life.
Proverbs 22:6

Fun

I think fun is on its way, Lord.
I'll enjoy climbing trees again,
peering at patterns in the bark;
I'll probe holes for insects,
and hide in the leaves.
I'll enjoy throwing a tennis ball as high as I can into
the sky
just as I used to when I was a child.
I'll teach my baby to roll a ball,
throw a ball,
and catch a ball.
I'll peer at caterpillars,
watch them arch their backs
and curl up into a circle.
I'll put a rose under my baby's nose
so he can smell its sweet fresh perfume.
I'll read *Thomas the Tank Engine*,
and make chuff-chuff noises.
I'll sing 'Humpty Dumpty'
and 'Row, row, row the boat'.
I have a feeling that it's all going to be great fun.

[Jesus said] 'You have trained children and
babies to offer perfect praise.'
Matthew 21:16

The mountains and hills will burst into singing,
and the trees will shout for joy.
Isaiah 55:12

The Lord will take delight in you,
and in his love he will give you new life.
He will sing and be joyful over you.
Zephaniah 3:17

Be glad, earth and sky! Roar, sea, and every creature
in you; be glad, fields, and everything in you!
The trees in the woods will shout for joy when
the Lord comes to rule the earth. He will rule the
peoples of the world with justice and fairness.
Psalm 96:11-13

Fill your minds with those things that are good and
that deserve praise: things that are true, noble,
right, pure, lovely, and honourable.
Philippians 4:8

One Day at a Time

Lord, right now I know that the best thing to do is
to take one day at a time,
even one hour at a time,
though, to be honest,
I don't have time to look at the clock
and certainly can't be governed by it
as I was at work.
I mustn't rush ahead in my thinking
because it's then that I start to panic
and wonder and worry.
Thank you for this moment.
Let me just be.
Be.

Help me to treasure the little things
that are good about having this little baby:
to see his sweet sleeping face,
to realise how he is completely dependent on me,
to have the joy of cuddling him.

Don't let me wish my time away.
Yes, I'm finding these first weeks tough,
but I want to savour each little bit of good that is
in them.

When my bones were being formed, carefully
put together in my mother's womb, when I was
growing there in secret, you knew that I was there –
you saw me before I was born. The days allotted
to me had all been recorded in your book,
before any of them ever began.

Psalm 139:15, 16

Before you created the hills or brought the world
into being, you were eternally God, and will be
God forever … A thousand years to you are like
one day; they are like yesterday, already gone,
like a short hour in the night.

Psalm 90:2, 4

Teach us how short our life is,
so that we may become wise.

Psalm 90:12

[Jesus said] 'Do not start worrying: "Where will my
food come from? or my drink? or my clothes?" …
Your Father in heaven knows that you need all these
things. Instead, be concerned above everything else
with the Kingdom of God and with what he requires
of you, and he will provide you with all these other
things. So do not worry about tomorrow; it will
have enough worries of its own. There is no need
to add to the troubles each day brings.'

Matthew 6:31-34

Returning to Work

I know I don't have to think of it yet, Lord,
but I wonder what I'll do about returning to work
or not.
These first few years of life are so precious
and so quickly gone
so I'm told.

I want to give my baby,
my toddler,
my growing child,
my turbulent teenager,
as much of my time and attention as she deserves.

I brought her into the world
and it's up to me to look after her
and I want to do a good job.
But it'll be tight financially if I stay at home.

Help me to consider the pros and cons
very carefully,
though at the moment that stage seems far off.

I don't know what lies ahead.
I trust you for today
and I trust you for what's to come.
Thank you for the way you've helped me in the past.
I rest in you.

Whatever you do, work at it with all your heart,
as though you were working for the Lord
and not for people.

Colossians 3:23

I alone know the plans I have for you,
plans to bring you prosperity and not disaster,
plans to bring about the future you hope for.

Jeremiah 29:11

We may make our plans, but God has the last word.
You may think everything you do is right,
but the Lord judges your motives.
Ask the Lord to bless your plans, and you
will be successful in carrying them out.

Proverbs 16:1-3

Thank You For My Baby

Thank you, Lord, for my baby.
She's lying in her cot at the moment,
dressed in her white Babygro
with a little white hat on her head
and I can hardly believe that I have a baby.
She looks like a doll
when she's at rest like this:
porcelain skin,
wispy hair,
long-lashed eyes,
tiny nose.
I keep looking at her
and thinking how the bump that was inside me
is now a live little girl for all to see.
I can see her chest rising
and falling
rhythmically,
gently,
a sign of life.

What a beautiful creation
you have made.
What a miracle
of ingenuity,
love,
and care
on your part.

I'm lost for words other than
'Thank you'.

When Elizabeth heard Mary's greeting, the baby
moved within her. Elizabeth was filled with the Holy
Spirit and said in a loud voice, 'You are the most
blessed of all women, and blessed is the child you
will bear! Why should this great thing happen to me,
that my Lord's mother comes to visit me?
For as soon as I heard your greeting, the baby
within me jumped with gladness.'

Luke 1:41-44

Sing to the Lord, all the world! Worship the Lord
with joy; come before him with happy songs!
Acknowledge that the Lord is God.
He made us, and we belong to him;
we are his people, we are his flock.

Psalm 100:1-3

God has made us what we are, and in our union
with Christ Jesus he has created us for a life of good
deeds, which he has already prepared for us to do.

Ephesians 2:10

Guardians of Treasure

Lord, thank you for entrusting this new little life to me.
How amazing: you think that we fallible,
fallen
human beings
are worthy of looking after
one of your most precious creations
on your behalf.

I wonder at your wisdom,
because we're not very good at
looking after your world.
Think of the African elephant,
the rain forests,
the wild flower species
that are disappearing
because we're not caring properly
for your world as you told us to.

And yet you entrust us
with the most valued pinnacle
of your creation, the human being.

It's humbling
and affirming
that you call us to be guardians
of this treasured being.
Help us to make a good job of it
and to be grateful to you
for your confidence in us.

Love the Lord your God and always obey all his
laws. Remember today what you have learned about
the Lord through your experiences with him ...
So then, obey the commands that I have given you
today; love the Lord your God and serve him with
all your heart ... Teach them to your children.
Talk about them when you are at home and
when you are away, when you are resting
and when you are working.

Deuteronomy 11:1, 2, 13, 19

Look out for one another's interests,
not just for your own.

Philippians 2:4

My Parents

Thank you for my parents, Lord.
They're so excited to be grandparents
and seem to be naturals at handling my baby
though they say they were completely ignorant
about babies
until they had their own.

They're candid with me
about their own efforts
at parenting.
They reckon they got some things right
and some things wrong.
They say I'll learn from their mistakes
and will vow not to follow their example,
but that I'll just make
different mistakes!

When I get uptight
and wonder if I'll ever get the hang of motherhood,
they reassure me
and say they were clueless to start with,
but to look at me now!

Dear friends, let us love one another, because love comes from God. Whoever loves is a child of God and knows God. Whoever does not love does not know God, for God is love. And God showed his love for us by sending his only Son into the world, so that we might have life through him.

1 John 4:7-9

I remember the sincere faith you have, the kind of faith that your grandmother Lois and your mother Eunice also had. I am sure that you have it also.

2 Timothy 1:5

For those who honour the Lord, his love lasts forever, and his goodness endures for all generations of those who are true to his covenant and who faithfully obey his commands.

Psalm 103:17, 18

First Smile

Joy, joy, joy! Guess what, Lord!
Our baby smiled today
for the first time,
and not a windy smile,
a proper smile.
He grinned a gummy grin
and moved his head
as if he wanted to giggle at us.
As well he might,
after the merry dance he's led us
over the last few weeks.
But if he thinks we're worth smiling at
maybe we're doing something right.

Thank you that he wants to communicate
with us and how much better is a smile
than a wail.
There have been times
when I haven't felt much like smiling
but I have a soppy grin all over my face
right now as I remember
that lovely baby smile
and know that we'll see it again
and again.
Joy, joy, joy indeed!

And it's just occurred to me, Lord,
that you talk about human beings

as your children.
So, as your child,
am I dependent on you
as my baby is on me?
Am I content in your presence,
as my baby is (most of the time) in mine?
And do I respond to your love for me
with a smile of happiness?

O Lord … your praise reaches up to the heavens;
it is sung by children and babies.
Psalm 8:1, 2

Lord, I have given up my pride and turned away
from my arrogance. I am not concerned with great
matters or with subjects too difficult for me. Instead,
I am content and at peace. As a child lies quietly in
its mother's arms, so my heart is quiet within me.
Psalm 131:1, 2

Emergency C-Section

'We need to hurry!'
That was the last thing I heard
before the anaesthetic knocked me out.
I was scared when they hit the red button
and whizzed me off to theatre.
I didn't want an emergency C-section,
but it was the only way in the end.

I have no recollection of the birth
of my baby
because I was out for the count.
I had to wait before meeting my little girl
and even then I was pretty blotto.

One thing I know:
it was such a relief
to see my baby and to know
that we were both alive.

It was worse for my partner,
having to sit waiting
to see if I was OK
while he held our baby.
He says that was such a special time
of daddy/daughter bonding
and praying that I'd make it too.

Thank you, Lord, that we came through it
and now we're three and back home.
My tummy is so sore
and I can't reach to pick my baby up from her cot,
but she's here,
alive and well,
and I'm thankful,
and so relieved.

I am in pain and despair; lift me up, O God,
and save me! I will praise God with a song;
I will proclaim his greatness by giving him thanks.
Psalm 69:29, 30

[Jesus said] 'When a woman is about to
give birth, she is sad because her hour of
suffering has come; but when the baby is born,
she forgets her suffering, because she is happy
that a baby has been born into the world.'
John 16:21

Early Arrival

My baby's come early, Lord,
so tiny,
so helpless,
so covered in tubes and monitoring devices.
Will she be all right?
Will she come through this trauma?

Thank you for the experts who are looking after her
while I watch,
powerless to do anything
other than talk to her
and talk to you about her.

You've brought her into the world, Lord,
and we will work with you
to do all we can to help her make it.
But you know that I'm scared, Lord.

When the waves of fear sweep over me,
keep me buoyant
and make me remember
that you are the one who stilled the water
in the fearful storm.
Please give me – and my husband
and our little baby
your peace.

Jesus said, 'Let the children come to me and
do not stop them, because the Kingdom of
heaven belongs to such as these.'
Matthew 19:14

I am always aware of the Lord's presence;
he is near, and nothing can shake me. And so I am
thankful and glad, and I feel completely secure.
Psalm 16:8, 9

Perfection

People talk about the perfection of babies, Lord,
but my little one is not perfect in the eyes of the
world.
She has disabilities
that will affect her for the rest of her life.
She may be ostracised by some people and bullied
by others.
Help me to remember
that she is precious in your sight,
that you love her just as she is
and that my love for her
is your love being passed on to her.
Thank you for giving me
the special privilege
and responsibility
of loving and caring for this baby.
Show me every day how I can love her
so that she knows my love
and your love for her.

'I am dedicating him to the Lord. As long as he lives,
he will belong to the Lord.'
1 Samuel 1:28

God purposely chose what the world considers
nonsense in order to shame the wise, and he chose
what the world considers weak in order to shame
the powerful. He chose what the world looks down
on and despises and thinks is nothing, in order to
destroy what the world thinks is important. This
means that no one can boast in God's presence.

1 Corinthians 1:27-29

See that you don't despise any of these little ones.
Their angels in heaven, I tell you, are always
in the presence of my Father in heaven.

Matthew 18:10

May you always be joyful in your union with the
Lord. I say it again: rejoice! Show a gentle attitude
toward everyone. The Lord is coming soon. Don't
worry about anything, but in all your prayers ask
God for what you need, always asking him with a
thankful heart. And God's peace, which is far beyond
human understanding, will keep your hearts and
minds safe in union with Christ Jesus.

Philippians 4:4-7

Adoption

At last, Lord!
The adoption has come through.
We've been deemed worthy
of having these two little people enter our lives.

You know, Lord, only too well,
how the years of waiting
and longing for a baby of our own,
came to nothing.
Our prayers weren't answered;
at least, not in the way we wanted.

But look at us now!
Two for the price of one!

It's weird to think that you've known them
since before they were born.
You know the circumstances
that led up to this brother and sister coming our way.
Help us to be good parents
and thank you for entrusting these special children
into our care.

Trust in the Lord with all your heart. Never rely on
what you think you know. Remember the Lord in
everything you do, and he will show you the right way.

Proverbs 3:5, 6

Every good gift and every perfect present
comes from heaven; it comes down from God,
the Creator of the heavenly lights, who does
not change or cause darkness by turning.

James 1:17

The CV of a One-Year-Old

I am only one
but I am one.

I can walk
– after a fashion.
My reversing skills are a bit suspect
and I sometimes miss
when I try to sit down.

I'm a good climber
onto the sofa or
up the stairs,
but not so good at
coming down,
down,
down:
bump.

I like to explore plant pots
and spread dusty compost
on the carpet
and swish it with my fingers.
If I'm caught at it
I smile
and refrain from doing what I shouldn't

till Mummy goes out of the room
and leaves me to my fun.
I can also
roll a ball and
knock beaker towers down
and cuddle my rag doll
and take Teddy for walks in his buggy.

I'm good at hiding from Mummy and Daddy
by putting my hands over my eyes.
I'm excellent at splashing in the bath,
doing high fives with my uncles,
taking things off the supermarket shelves,
and eating chocolate buttons.

Pretty good for one year on the planet.

My parents like to think
it's their doing. Huh!

I am only one
but I am one.

Also available in the series

HELP! I'm a New Dad!
1501555

You'll find a large collection of David's books at
www.kevinmayhew.com